BECOMING

A

SOMEBODY

THE STORY OF
GIDEON
OF MANASSEH

NICHOLAS E. HARRIS

Copyright © 1999

Published by Ariel Ministries
Edmond, Oklahoma

Scripture quotations are from the King James Version of the Bible.

Library of Congress Card Number: 99-94382
ISBN: 0-7392-0206-5

Cover design by Laura A. Alfonzo

Additional copies may be obtained by writing to the following address:
Dr. Nicholas E. Harris
Ariel Ministries
P.O. Box 3616
Edmond, OK 73083-3616

Becoming A Somebody may be obtained by retail outlets at special rates.
Write to the above address for more information.

Printed in the USA by Morris Publishing, 3212 East Highway 30, Kearney, NE 68847

Contents

Introduction v

Step 1 . . . . "Assess Your Values" 1

Step 2 . . . . "Forget the Crowd and Watch the Enemy" 19

Step 3 . . . . "Be Vigilant" 27

Step 4 . . . . "Obey the Divine Directive" 37

Step 5 . . . . "Stand Your Ground" 51

Introduction

HAVE YOU EVER had the awful feeling that if you disappeared from the face of the earth, no one would miss you? Millions of people experience the same emotion of insecurity, inferiority, or low self-esteem. Regardless of the name, it makes people miserable.

I know all about feelings of inferiority and low self-esteem. As a teenager and young adult, I fought endless battles against feelings of inadequacy. My self-image was horrible. Negativity governed my life. I felt like I was a NOBODY. I could not force myself to apply for a job, ask a girl for a date, or appear in a school play, all because of a totally distorted view of myself. My lack of understanding about God's investment in me resulted in this warped point of view.

However, that changed. I began to see myself as God sees me and my entire life was transformed. For the first time, I experienced a sense of significance and purpose. The excitement of this sense of meaning and direction never ceases. Since that day, I eagerly share my experience with others suffering from insecurity. I hope you discover what I discovered: I found the SOME-BODY God created me to be. It can happen to you, too!

To aid in this discovery effort, I have identified five simple steps to a more abundant and joyful way of living. I believe anyone taking these five steps can be transformed from a NOBODY into a SOMEBODY.

I first discovered these steps over thirty years ago while reading the book of Judges. I read the story of Gideon ben Joash, with whom I totally identified. Gideon saw himself as a NOBODY. However, by taking these same five steps, Gideon was transformed into a SOMEBODY. These steps provide everything you need to make the same transition. This may be Gideon's story, but it can be your story.

s t e p
1

Assess
Your
Values

GIDEON BEN JOASH lived during a period when he
and his countrymen were in great peril. This is odd,
since Israel should have been prospering. After all, they
were dwelling in Canaan, the land God had promised to
give them. One hundred years before Gideon's birth, his
predecessors conquered Canaan under the leadership of
the great Joshua ben Nun. All the land from Dan to
Beer-sheba belonged to the children of Israel. However,
by the time Gideon ben Joash became a man, Israel faced
a real national crisis. Portions of their land were under
assault by aggressive nomadic people from the deserts of

Transjordan, the Midianites. As a result, Israelite control of Canaan became tenuous at best, especially in the northern part of the country. This circumstance was not a coincidence; the Midianites were in this land for a reason. According to the book of Judges, God allowed this oppressive state of affairs to develop. The text states:

> "... they (the people of Israel) did what was evil in the sight of the Lord." (Judges 6:1)

Israel faced trouble because God's protection no longer encompassed them; they had removed themselves from God's protective oversight by choosing to turn their backs on Him and live in sin. They willingly entangled themselves in a transgression God hates above all others — idolatry. The people of Israel rejected the God of Abraham, Isaac, and Jacob and aligned themselves with the fertility gods of the Canaanites, in particular the god known as Baal.

God hated Baal just as He hates all false gods. He never shares allegiance with any god people imagine or fashion for themselves. God always withdraws Himself from those worshiping false gods. When God withdraws His presence He also takes His protective covering, just as He did in the days of Gideon ben Joash.

Why does God hate idolatry? The Bible has a clear answer. God hates the worship of idols because it cripples His people. It cripples them morally, and it cripples them relationally. All forms of sin cripple

2

people, but idolatry goes one step further. It leads its
worshipers into bondage. Bondage and idolatry go hand
in hand. Wherever and whenever people worship
created things, they fall into a state of servitude. The
examples are endless, but the experiences of Israel are
classic.

Long before the days of Gideon, God showed Israel
the connection between idolatry and servitude. In fact,
as soon as Israel arrived at Mount Sinai, God said:

> **"I am the LORD thy God, which have
> brought thee out of the land of Egypt, out
> of the house of bondage; therefore (be-
> cause that is so . . . because I have set you
> free) thou shalt have no other gods before
> me."** (Exodus 20:2-3)

This declaration from the mouth of God was not
only an ultimatum, it was also a teaching tool. It demonstrated His love of freedom and His hatred of bondage. Over the centuries, God reiterates His unrestrained
love of freedom again and again. He has never equivo-
cated. The thing that sets our God apart from all the
other gods (little "g") is His determination to liberate the
captives and free the oppressed. In this, God is unique.
All other gods bring bondage to people. They enslave
because their worshipers bring religious trappings with
them. These gods, by their very nature, are religious.
However, God has never been religious. He is relational.

The word religious is important to this story. It
comes from the word "religion," which has an interesting

etymology. It is derived from the Latin noun
RELIGARE. The prefix RE means "to turn toward" and
the root LIGARE means "to bind." So the definition of
the word religion is "to turn oneself toward bondage."
That is what religion does. It binds. It places people in
chains.

God detests religion. Religion brings bondage. He
prefers relationship over the practice of religion because
relationship brings freedom. Israel should have known
this. While dwelling in Egypt, a land filled with religion
and idols, they experienced nothing but servitude and
bondage. Once they followed their God out of Egypt,
they became a free people.

Since God wanted Israel to remain free, He gave
them the instructions recorded in Exodus 20:2-3. The
wording is very interesting. God says:

> "I *am* the LORD thy God, which have
> brought thee out of the land of Egypt, out
> of the house of bondage. Thou shalt have
> no other gods before me."

In other words, "You are now a free people. If you
want to remain free, you shall not have any gods standing before Me."

What is interesting is what God did not say. He did
not tell Israel, "You shall have no other gods." He
simply forbid the people of Israel to elevate the value of
other gods until they threatened the place reserved for
Him alone.

What are some of these other gods? Any cherished

material object has the potential to become a god to us, especially those things which bring meaning and purpose to our lives. Any of these things can be elevated to a place of worship. Jobs, homes, children, and even churches can become gods. These things are not evil in and of themselves, nor does God forbid His people to value these things; but God does forbid His people to worship these things.

The worship of material things is what turns a god into an idol. Our gods are the things we value, while our idols are the things we worship. In fact, any god can become an idol if we elevate it to the source of all meaning and value in our lives. It becomes an idol when it is placed before God.

Money, for example, is a very valuable thing. It is difficult to live without. Money can become so important we cannot live meaningfully without an overabundance of it. When that occurs, money becomes an idol. It becomes an object to be worshiped. We can elevate our children to the level of idols. We can become so devoted to our children that when they mature and leave home, our lives appear meaningless and empty. Any material object can be elevated to the place of worship and be an idol in our lives. Many of us slip into the worship of things, from time to time, without even knowing it. When we do, servitude always follows.

The end result of Israel's flirtation with Baal provides a classic example of the enslaving capabilities of idolatry. Baal belonged to a category of idols known as fertility

5

gods. What attracted people to the worship of these fertility gods was their perceived ability to provide material blessings. People believed Baal and the other fertility gods would provide more children, more livestock, and bigger crops in return for their worship. For centuries on end, people worshiped these fertility gods shaped by mortal hands from pieces of metal or stone. In the case of Baal, the artisans shaped him to resemble a powerful bull, the epitome of strength and male virility. But he was only a "hunk of junk"; he was lifeless.

The fact is none of our gods have life — none of them possess eternal life. Only God possesses eternal life. All gods are composed of material substances. Whether metallic or of flesh and blood, they are all subject to decay and erosion. That includes those made of precious materials like gold. All idols are temporal in nature, not eternal. Temporal things have no power because they cannot provide a basis for absolute values. Only a timeless God in possession of an eternal life force can provide a true basis for absolute and everlasting values.

That is why, over the centuries, societies engaging in idolatry view themselves as NOBODIES. If their gods (things they consider to be of ultimate value) decay, their moral value as gods is worthless; eventually their gods have no value. If their gods are worthless, so are they. They see themselves as having no more real value than the animals. With no hope of eternity for either their gods or themselves, people feel empty. They fill their lives with mood-altering drugs, pursue sensual pleasures, and acquire more and more material things to hide their hopelessness. Idolaters may give the appearance of being happy, but deep down inside they are an empty void because they have no future; and they know it.

The temptation to worship idols is aroused in us by social pressure. When significant others in our lives or a significant majority of those around us practice some form of idolatry, it becomes very difficult for us to resist. The excuse is usually that everybody else does it, which was exactly the excuse put forward by the people of Israel. Once they settled themselves in Canaan, they were tempted to worship Baal since everybody else did. Baal was a god they could see and touch. People have always found it easier to worship a visible god than to worship the invisible God, Yahweh of Israel.

At first, Israel resisted the idolatrous pressures. The longer they dwelled in Canaan the more these pressures increased, until the people began to assimilate Canaanite values and attitudes. Eventually, they adopted portions of the idolatrous Canaanite religious rituals and worshiped at the shrines of Baal. When they did, they exchanged their relationship with the one true God for the religion of Canaan. Overnight the freedom they had known since the days of the exodus was forfeited for a life of bondage.

Seeing the growing idolatrous condition of His people, God sent a prophet to speak to them. He said:

"... **Thus saith the LORD God of Israel,**

> I brought you up from Egypt, and brought
> you forth out of the house of bondage;
> And I delivered you out of the hand of the
> Egyptians, and out of the hand of all that
> oppressed you, and drave them out from
> before you, and gave you their land . . ."
> "And I said unto you, I am the LORD
> your God; fear not the gods of the
> Amorites, in whose land ye dwell: but ye
> have not obeyed my voice." (Judges 6:8b-
> 10)

The words of the prophet are chilling, especially in
context. This unnamed prophet reminded the sons of
Israel of their condition prior to the exodus. They had
been oppressed bondservants in Egypt when their great
God came and set them free. Then, as if that were not
enough, He gave them all the land of Canaan as their
inheritance.

Now, only seventy years later, they turned from their
God to worship this false god Baal. As a result, they were
oppressed by the nomadic Midianites. The invaders
stripped them of every vestige of self-worth and human
dignity. But God was prepared to reclaim what His
people had sacrificed in their flirtation with Baal. When
the time was right, He sent an angel to initiate His plan
of redemption.

Prior to dispatching this angel, God selected a man
to serve as His personal instrument. The man is our
hero, Gideon ben Joash. The angel found the son of
Joash hiding in an underground wine press, winnowing
his wheat. He had hidden himself, hoping the
Midianites would not find him, because he knew they

would steal what little grain he had.

Needless to say, in this condition Gideon did not look like a savior — he looked like a coward. But God has never been concerned with outward appearances. God is concerned with the hearts of men. He searches for the possibilities hidden within the souls of people, not their liabilities. The angel of the Lord addressed Gideon as God saw him, not as Gideon saw himself or as others saw him. The name the angel used must have staggered Gideon. He said:

> "The Lord is with thee, THOU MIGHTY MAN OF VALOR." (Judges 6:12)

How humorous! To call this man, hiding in a wine press, a mighty man of valor was a joke. He looked like a "scaredy-cat." But the Angel of the Lord, someone who knows, refers to him as a "mighty man of valor." The angel spoke in the language of possibilities. He saw a "mighty man of valor" lurking inside Gideon just waiting to be released. Of course, this was not the first time God addressed the hidden potential in a most unlikely person, and it would not be the last. Throughout history God has majored in the development of untapped talent, and He often finds these people in unlikely places. He found one of the world's greatest prophets working in a fig orchard. He found a future king herding jackasses, and he found a deliverer for His people hiding in a wine press.

If Gideon had such enormous potential, what caused

his self-image to be so distorted? Judges provides a clear answer. Gideon's negative image of himself was generated, at least in part, by several warped ideas Gideon had adopted from his cultural surroundings. One of those twisted ideas involved material wealth. Gideon, like many people today, believed the only people who really counted were those with wealth. Gideon revealed this twisted concept when replying to the messenger of the Lord:

> **"Oh my Lord, wherewith shall I save Israel? Behold, my family is POOR in Manasseh and I am the LEAST in my father's house."** (Judges 6:15) *(emphasis mine)*

This statement makes it clear Gideon determined his self-image and self-esteem from what he owned. Since he considered himself a poor man from a poor family, he referred to himself as "the least in his father's house." In other words, he was the least adequate of all his inadequate relatives. In his own eyes he was a NOBODY. Without question, Baal worship contributed to his lack of self-worth. When we worship gods made of gold, gold is all that counts. Gideon had no gold.

Fortunately for Gideon, God has never been a materialist. He has never cared what people have or do not have. In His eyes greatness is never attached to a person's possessions. He looks at what a person can become, not what they have. So when God looked at Gideon, He ignored his poverty. God saw Gideon's potential.

Bringing this potential to the surface was the real challenge God faced with Gideon. When a person's self-image is as distorted as Gideon's, it needs massive reprogramming. Without this reprogramming, God knew Gideon would never accept or develop his potential. The negativity of Gideon at this point in his life was monumental. Gideon simply could not accept the angel's reference as "a mighty man of valor." He did not believe he was mighty, nor did he believe he could become a man of valor.

Apparently, Gideon knew very little about the principles of faith. His own self-confidence was so weak he could not conceive of being useful to anyone, much less the God of Abraham. So, in total disbelief, Gideon asked the Angel of the Lord to provide a sign to prove this whole episode was not just his imagination.

This request for a sign offers proof positive that if Gideon ever had a faith thought, he never walked by it. By definition, faith is "**the substance of things hoped for, the evidence of things NOT SEEN**" (Hebrews 11:1). Therefore, true faith does not ask for signs in order to believe. The request to be shown a sign indicates Gideon did not understand the first thing about walking by faith.

Over the centuries, God resists requests for signs because He knows the appearance of a sign rarely leads people to real faith. However, God's great concern for the plight of His people and their desperate need for a dynamic leader, prompted God to allow Gideon ben Joash to test Him — and Gideon did, twice.

The first sign was pivotal. The Angel of God caused fire to come from a rock and devour several cakes and a few pieces of meat. This may be the only occasion in the biblical record where a visible sign enabled a person to believe. This sign provided Gideon with enough inner strength to take one small step of faith. Evidently, when Gideon saw fire come from a rock, something began to stir within his soul. All those inferiority feelings began to evaporate. They had not vanished, but they were going. Gideon was on the road to becoming a SOMEBODY. But to fully attain the ultimate goal God had established for his life, Gideon was required to obey several divine directives.

The first directive was the most difficult. It not only required great obedience, but great courage. Through the angelic messenger, God told Gideon:

> ". . . pull down the altar of Baal which your father has, and cut down the Asherah that is beside it, and build in its place an altar to the Lord your God." (Judges 6:25-26)

12

To obey this divine demand was risky business, and Gideon knew it. Baalism was entrenched and sacrosanct among some Israelites, including Gideon's father, Joash. Defiling this idol could cost Gideon his life. However, since God told him to destroy his idol, Gideon accepted the risk. If Gideon and his people were to reclaim their land and their liberty, this Baal and all the other Baals had to be destroyed. Gideon was wise enough to understand the destruction of these idols needed to be initiated in his own household. If he was to be the liberator of God's people, he must lift the standard. To allow Baal to stand in his own home while condemning others was hypocritical. The Baal of Joash had to be destroyed.

However, the destruction of the idol itself was not all that had to happen. This idol and the grove surrounding it was only a symptom of a greater disease. The disease involved elevated temporal values which gave expression to this idol. These, too, had to be destroyed.

The destruction of Baal was not all God asked of Gideon. It was only the first step. God knew that Gideon's actions would lead him into a life of faith. Every walk of faith takes place one step at a time. For example, the great Methodist evangelist John Wesley said he was a believer and a minister of the gospel for many years before he experienced the reality of mountain-moving faith. During that faithless period, rather than dwelling upon his doubt, Wesley kept preaching faith. After a while he experienced faith for himself. Wesley took the first step by proclaiming the reality of faith and found himself walking by faith. What had begun in him as a mustard seed, a simple word, eventually became a great tree.

That is how Gideon began his journey of faith. His first step was to destroy his father's Baal as God commanded. Gideon's faith was infantile at that juncture,

13

because he acted in the dead of night. A fully developed faith responds in the full light of day. Gideon did not yet possess full-grown faith, so he waited until everyone was sleeping. Judges 6:27 tells us why:

> "... he was too afraid of his father's household and the men of the city to do it by day."

However, to Gideon's credit, he refused to allow his fears to stop him from obeying God. In fact, Judges 6:27 states:

> "Then Gideon took ten men of his servants AND DID AS THE LORD HAD SPOKEN." *(emphasis mine)*

In spite of his insecurities and inner fear, Gideon chose to act. He slipped into the grove of trees where Baal stood and destroyed the grove and the idol. This pleased God, and He rewarded Gideon's obedience by promoting feelings of self-worth in his soul.

The same is true of any who dare to obey God today. If we take the time to search out the will of God and act upon its instructions, negativity and inadequacy begin to erode, especially when obedience leads to the destruction of our idols. Remember, any valued thing which stands above God in our lives must be smashed. Once these idols are destroyed, we can do what Gideon did. He immediately replaced the idol with an altar to the one true God, an altar he called "Jehovah Shalom" which means "The Peace of God." Once we have destroyed our idols, we are free to establish an altar to the one true

God. When we do this, we begin to experience "Jehovah Shalom," the peace of God. We begin to believe what the apostle Paul said:

> **"I can do all things through Christ who strengthens me."** (Philippians 4:13)

I experienced a Gideon-type idol smashing. On April 11, 1969, I surrendered to the call God placed upon my life. I had been in rebellion against God, worshiping at the altar of a Baal. Day in and day out I bowed my knees before material objects. As a result, I became quite wealthy at a very young age.

On the surface it appeared the gods I worshiped had been very good to me. At twenty-eight years of age I enjoyed an annual income of $48,000+ (a lot of money in 1969). I amassed all the grown-up toys people around me broke their necks to secure. But I discovered that my gods were not as good to me as I thought. In fact, these materialistic gods robbed me of my essential meaning and purpose. I was not a free man. My idols constantly prodded me to accumulate more and more things. To meet their demands, I gave them more and more of myself. In time, I had such a thirst for material things I could not rest. I had no inner peace.

Since my gods were both temporal and material in nature, my personal and moral values reflected them. My values became temporal and material. Like Gideon, my image was based on the things I possessed rather than the person I was made to be. To improve my

15

image, I continued to amass more and more things, but they never satisfied my gods or myself.

When God sent His grace to me in April of 1969, my life was in chaos. I soon discovered God did not care about the mess. He chose to ignore my glaring weaknesses. He moved into the meaningless void of my life. When He did, He replaced my tyrannical, self-destructive, materialistic "gods" with His own loving spirit. I suddenly knew my real worth to Him, a worth not based upon things. It was based upon my personhood. I am now a child of God — I have been born of Him and that is why I have value to God. Any child of God is a SOMEBODY. God says that in every page of the New Testament. I am a SOMEBODY, not based on what I have, but based on who I am. My old gods never said that. They always said, "You are a NOBODY unless you have things." God whispered to me, "You are a SOMEBODY because you are my child." I believed Him.

So on April 11, 1969, I chose to leave my $48,000 job to become a Methodist pastor. My annual salary was reduced by 90%, but that did not matter to me. Like Gideon of old, I took the axe of obedience and destroyed the altar of Baal in my heart. For the first time in my life, I was a free man. I knew what Jesus meant when He said:

> **"If the Son therefore shall make you free, ye shall be free indeed."** (John 8:36)

However, I did not stop with destroying the Baals in

my heart. Just like Gideon, I began to chop down the grove surrounding my altar. The grove represented all those things which the Baal in my heart demanded, things like houses, cars, jewelry, and money. Once I had destroyed all those things, my life had new meaning and direction. Temporal things no longer dominated my life. Even though I did not know it at the time, I was well on my way to becoming a SOMEBODY. I took step one, the same step Gideon of Manasseh took. I tore down my idols.

Anyone desiring to make the journey to becoming a SOMEBODY must take this step. All idols must be eliminated; then you will be ready to consider the second step.

Becoming A Somebody

.
.
.
.
18 .
.
.
.

step

2

Forget the Crowd and Watch the Enemy

WHILE GIDEON WAS called and equipped as a "mighty man of valor" to liberate His people, Satan was not idle. He organized his resistance to God's plan. His weapon was desert invaders. Up to this time, the Midianites and Amalekites had only conducted periodic incursions into Galilee. But as Gideon took his first step, Satan sent one hundred fifty thousand warriors into the Jezreel Valley. The sudden appearance of so many enemy warriors must have challenged the emerging faith of Gideon to the very core! Gideon had only two options. He could continue to walk in his newly acquired faith or he could fall back into fear and despair. Gideon made the right choice. He chose to walk by faith, not by sight (I Corinthians 5:7).

Gideon discovered it was easier to take the second step of faith than the first. After all, Gideon now had some faith experience to assist him. Every person I have ever known who walks by faith testifies that the more they walk by faith the easier that walk becomes.

I experienced this same phenomena myself. Soon after my own conversion experience, I read 1 Corinthians 5:7. I understood God wanted me to walk by faith, not by sight, so I began to step out. At first, my walk was a bit feeble, but I did not let my weaknesses stop me. I had taken my first step of faith. I left my job and entered the full-time ministry. As a second step, I started to pray for the lost, the sick, and the relationally impaired. Like Abraham of old, I began to speak of things that are not as though they were (Romans 4:17). To my delight, people began to be saved, healed and restored. With this step behind me, I took a third step. I resisted temptation and challenged Satan in the name of Jesus. Satan started to flee from me. As more victories were gained, I grew stronger and eager to walk further.

The same was true of Gideon. By faith he chose to believe the God who made the heavens and earth was on his side. Certain God's power stood behind him, he determined to do combat with any and all enemies of God, regardless of their number. This decision to engage

the enemy constituted Gideon's second major step of
faith. Only faith enabled this man to believe he could
lead a people like Israel against one hundred fifty thousand invaders and be victorious.

Once Gideon took this second step, his faith
strengthened. Something changed the entire course of
Gideon's life. Judges 6:34 declares:

> " . . . the power of God came upon
> Gideon." (Judges 6:34)

The text does not indicate how the power of God
descended upon Gideon, only that it did. When that
power came, Gideon was transformed. He might have
been frightened, but he would never again be a coward.
Spiritually quickened and vitally alive, Gideon picked up
the reins of leadership. He assumed the role of the
shepherd of the flock of Israel. His first act was to
summon the men of Israel to battle. Within hours,
thousands of warriors reported for duty. This response
seems odd, since Gideon was relatively unknown at the
time. He had no leadership experience. This great
response to his summons demonstrates what I consider
to be a most important spiritual truth: if one solitary
person steps out in faith and challenges the enemy of
God, thousands will rally to that person's side.

Once again the experiences of Wesley provide an
excellent example of this phenomenon. In the 1730s,
after experiencing his famous "heart warming" at a
prayer meeting on Aldersgate Street, he preached the

gospel with such fervor and excitement the hierarchy of the Church of England felt threatened. They banned him from the pulpits of the local church parishes of England and Wales.

However, Wesley would not allow the disfavor of a spiritually bankrupt ecclesiastical leadership to silence or discourage him. Although banned from the pulpits of England, he refused to stop preaching. He simply consecrated the fields of Britain to be his sanctuary and tree stumps to be his pulpit. Before John Wesley died fifty years later, a million people called themselves Methodist and stood at Wesley's side.

The awesome American evangelist Dwight L. Moody provides another example of this spiritual truth. This courageous man stepped into the streets of Chicago, Illinois, where he single-handedly confronted crime, degradation, and poverty in the name of Jesus Christ. This one man had the faith to challenge the forces of Satan to hand-to-hand combat. By the time Moody finished his course on this earth, hundreds of thousands of men, women, and children became warriors in the Kingdom of God.

The examples of this phenomena are unending, and the facts are incontestable. Whenever and wherever people decide to stand their ground for God, they do not stand alone very long. Others always join their cause.

When Gideon's summons went out, thirty-two thousand men reported to do battle with the Midianite invaders. Such an enthusiastic response must have been

a great morale booster for Gideon, but God was not
particularly impressed. Great numbers can be deceitful.
Before the day was over, God taught Gideon the
unimportance of huge crowds: God instructed Gideon
to send the majority of these thirty-two thousand men
back to their homes. God wanted Gideon to understand
He has never required an enormous number of people to
accomplish a task. As the prophet, Zechariah, would
later say, "**Not by might, nor by power, but by My
spirit, saith the LORD of hosts**" (Zechariah 4:6).
History demonstrates when God has one man, He does
the most amazing things. Gideon learned this truth and
so did the entire nation of Israel. God taught them by
drastically pruning their army.

The pruning began when God told Gideon to send
home every fearful man. Within minutes, two-thirds of
Gideon's army deserted him. Gideon's fighting force was
reduced from 32,000 to 10,000. Without question, he
was totally baffled by this divine directive. As he sur-
veyed the ten thousand remaining soldiers, he must have
had some questions for God, one question being:
"Why?" He asked this question because he did not
know the things an omniscient God knows. The depar-
ture of these 22,000 men enhanced Gideon's chances of
victory. God knew what their fear would do. It is always
a deterrent to victory. In any form of combat, fear
constitutes a liability. It is rarely an asset. Men who fear
injury, or capture, or death allow their fear to infect
other soldiers. The Bible makes it clear; fear is a detri-

23

ment to God's cause. God's word says, **"God has not given us a spirit of fear . . ."** (II Timothy 1:7). Fear, especially spiritual fear, is never from God.

Every person fighting a battle at God's side hears a voice in his or her head whispering, "Why are you here? Who do you think you are? You can't contribute a thing to God's cause. You are a NOBODY, you always have been. Why would God want you?" That voice we hear is not the voice of God, because the word of God assures us He does not give His people a spirit of fear.

When I first chose to answer the call to the ministry, I faced my own struggle with fear. The night before I preached my first sermon, the voice of fear whispered, "How dare you attempt to preach to these people! Who do you think you are to tell other people how to live their lives?" Fortunately, six days earlier I had heard a sermon from II Timothy 1:7 which says, **"God has not given us a spirit of fear ..."** So when I heard this inner voice questioning my abilities, I knew it could not be the voice of God. Because I knew the word of God, I also knew this was the voice of Satan trying to intimidate and confuse me.

My spirit arose in me and I rejected the satanic suggestion that I had no business preaching. The next morning I stood boldly behind the pulpit and spoke with courage. As I did, the power and strength of the Holy Spirit came upon me. I had not only chosen to reject those inner fears of the night before, but I had also proven to God and myself that I was willing to stand all alone with God if necessary. I would even become a fool if the circumstances warranted it. Most of all, as I stood behind that sacred desk for the first time, I ceased being a spiritual spectator and became an actual player in the game. God does not need a crowd to win a battle. He only needs one person willing to take a stand; together with that person, God wins the most resounding victories.

When Gideon allowed 22,000 men to return home, he demonstrated his willingness to be God's man. Though Satan gathered one hundred fifty thousand Midianites and Amalekites, Gideon would fight. He would not tremble. He understood God would rather have ten thousand men willing to trust Him than thirty-two thousand faithless and fearful men. God calls His people to depend upon Him, not numbers. When Gideon chose to put his total trust in God, he took the second step to becoming a SOMEBODY. Any person who stands alone at God's side is a real SOMEBODY.

3

Be
Vigilant

WHEN GOD TOLD Gideon to send 22,000 of his
men home, it must have been a real shocker. The shock
got worse. Even though He sent two-thirds of the army
home, God was not through pruning this army. Gideon
had another lesson to learn. God taught Gideon that the
elimination of fear and refusal to rely on a crowd were
not enough to guarantee complete victory. It has always
required more than fearlessness to become a SOME-
BODY.

To teach Gideon this next lesson, God told him to

send the ten thousand to a nearby stream to drink. As
these ten thousand men knelt beside the stream, God
gave Gideon a new directive. He told Gideon to sepa-
rate those men who were lying on their stomachs to
drink from those who were drinking water on their
knees. Gideon found 9,700 men lying on their stomachs, while only three hundred knelt beside the stream.
God instructed Gideon to dismiss all those on their
stomachs, and Gideon obeyed. Judges 7:8 states:

> ". . . and he sent all the rest of Israel every
> man unto his tent, and retained those three
> hundred men."

One might ask, "What on earth was wrong with
lying on one's stomach to get a drink?" The answer is
nothing is wrong with drinking on one's stomach. The
real issue is not how a man drinks water, but whether he
maintains a state of constant vigilance. Alertness and
preparedness are essential for soldiers in the army of the
Lord. God approved of those three hundred men
because they kept their heads up. They were in a position
to look for their enemies. They were vigilant. The apostle
Peter once issued this warning:

> "Be sober, be vigilant; because your ad-
> versary the devil, as a roaring lion, walketh
> about, seeking whom he may devour." (1
> Peter 5:8)

According to Peter, soldiers of God must constantly
be vigilant because their enemy, Satan, never ceases in his
efforts to devour them. Satan often tries to devour his

adversaries by arousing feelings of fearfulness and insecurity in them. Constant vigilance is required to keep these deep-seated inferiority feelings from being revived. These feelings can be rejuvenated more quickly than any other emotion we experience because negative input has been programmed into most of us from the moment we took our first breath.

I know about this struggle and the need for vigilance from personal experience. When I left adolescence and became an adult, I brought a tremendous emotional load with me. My subconscious mind contained hundreds of tapes labeled <u>INADEQUACY</u>, and many of these tapes were inadvertently programmed into me by my own father. My father was one of those men who gave very little positive input to his children. I am not suggesting he was abusive in any way. He was not. However, like most other men of his generation, he often tried to use negative input to motivate his children, especially me. As I grew up, nothing I did seemed to satisfy him. Every effort I made was just a little short of his expectations. Failure was programmed into me. As a result, I muddled through childhood and adolescence feeling totally inadequate. I performed according to what I was programmed to believe about myself — that I could never do anything right, so why try. As a rule, I underachieved in almost everything I attempted.

This predisposition to underachievement revealed itself in my academic efforts or lack thereof. When I made a good grade, my father never praised me. He only reacted when my grades were poor, and that was most of the time. He tried to motivate me in school by belittling me. When I brought home a D or an F, he called me ignorant and accused me of being lazy. Because of his constant negative input, I took less and less interest in academics. When I graduated from high school, I finished thirty-third academically in a class of fifty-five. Sadly enough, I was not at all disturbed by my poor showing; deep down inside I believed myself to be stupid. Logic told me stupid people make poor grades and graduate at the bottom of their class.

However, there were signs to suggest this negative evaluation of my intellectual abilities was totally wrong. For example, in the late 1950s, all high school juniors going to public school took the Iowa silent reading test. When the test was completed, I scored in the top two percent of all students that year. Someone should have realized the potential those test scores revealed, but no one did. As a matter of fact, one of my high school teachers, totally ignoring these exams, told me to learn a trade because I would never be able to graduate from college. As far as she was concerned I was a failure, and I was all too willing to accept her assessment. After all, since she was a high school teacher, she should know.

However, this overwhelming negative attitude was soon to change drastically. About a month after graduating, a college football coach offered me a scholarship to play football and baseball. My family and I immediately accepted the offer. When the fall semester began, I performed well as an athlete. Not surprisingly, however, I immediately began to fulfill everyone's expectations of me academically. That first college semester I made two Cs and three Ds. After all, a person like me, a person of limited intelligence and ability, is a C or D student. I expected nothing more of myself.

One fateful day this whole pattern of performance was interrupted. A psychology professor who loved athletics and attended our practices every day watched me perform. This professor was extremely observant. He saw things in me other people did not see. He noticed I played football in a state of anger, even in practice. Some people thought I was vicious; others accused me of playing "dirty."

This psychology professor did not believe the person he saw on the field was the real me. Behind all that aggression he saw a frightened child, not a vicious person; so one day after practice, he approached me and asked if I would visit with him in his office. I was curious, so I made an appointment. When I arrived at his office, I had barely sat down when he said to me, "Nick, why do you feel so worthless and inferior?"

I was shocked. I had never been consciously aware of any feelings of worthlessness and inferiority, so my first response was to reject his suggestion out of hand. But this man would not back away. He got in my face. He challenged me to be open with him and I could not resist. Over the next several months, this man spent much of his free time delving into my personality. Ever so gradually he opened the door to my subconscious mind. He brought to the surface hurts and pain which had poisoned my personality for over seventeen years. As this door opened, light flooded my inner recesses. The process of transforming me from a confirmed NOBODY into accepting myself as a SOMEBODY began. For the first time in my life, I began to face my inner fears. With the help of my friend, I finally understood these fears provoked crippling feelings of inferiority and prevented me from realizing my full potential. In time I controlled these fears and began to focus on my potential rather than my failures.

This was a great step forward, but my mentor did not stop at this point. He then taught me the same lesson God taught Gideon. He taught me the necessity of being constantly vigilant. He warned me these negative emotions would come back if I was not continually on guard.

As I began to understand the emotions causing these devastating feelings of inadequacy in my psyche, I discovered I could lift those emotions out of the realm of the subconscious and bring them into consciousness. When I did, I could see these feelings for what they actually were and deal with them in a constructive rather than a destructive way. Once I was able to identify what I was feeling and why, I found I could subdue many of those self-destructive feelings.

I caution you, negative emotions will not just disappear. We must be constantly vigilant. They will linger in our subconscious minds waiting for an opportunity to assault us. But once these negative emotions are properly identified, they can be addressed succinctly.

I can never thank this professor and friend enough for what he did for me. He not only taught me how to recognize the emotions, he also taught me to rapidly identify the areas of inner hurt giving rise to each negative emotion. Since those days so long ago, I have put into practice everything I was taught. Now I am constantly vigilant. Whenever a negative emotion arises from my subconscious mind, I can immediately identify that emotion.

This professor friend also taught me the importance of controlling my imagination. He helped me throw my negative emotions to the ground by chaining my imagination. In fact, one day he shared a mind-boggling truth. He told me the subconscious mind functions like a great stronghold, a fortress where the uncontrolled imagination can run rampant within the walls. Then he opened a Bible and read to me these words:

> **"For though we walk in the flesh, we do not war after the flesh: (For the weapons of our warfare are not carnal, but mighty through God to the pulling down of strongholds;) Casting down imaginations, and every high thing that exalteth itself against the knowledge of God, and bringing into captivity every thought to the obedience of Christ. . ."** (2 Corinthians 10:3-5)

33

Because I was not a Christian at that time, I had

difficulty understanding these words. That is no longer the case. Success in our continuing war to become somebodies requires the conquest of our imaginations. Under the guidance of this godly man, I went to war. I challenged my imagination and learned to cast it down. I achieved victory over my negative self-image, but only because a man of God cared enough to teach me how to destroy all those strongholds in my mind. Through his instruction, the entire direction of my life was altered, especially in the area of academics. In fact, after that first dismal semester, I eventually completed eleven years of college work, earning four degrees. In all those years I made only three Bs; all my other grades were As.

As the years passed, I became more skillful in the art of casting down inner fears. By exercising constant vigilance, I am able to keep most of those fears from returning. Constant vigilance is the key — just as it was the key for Gideon ben Joash and his little group of warriors. God allowed Gideon to keep those three hundred warriors because God knew these men were vigilant. God knew these men would stand their ground in the face of their enemy, even if they had to stand alone. We know this to be true because when 31,700 others left them to fight alone, they did not retreat. They refused to follow the crowd. They knew that sometimes a person has to stand alone to be victorious in life.

Those three hundred men, waiting to do battle at Gideon's side, recognized the odds. They knew they were vastly outnumbered. Judges 7:12 says the

Midianites were " . . . **like grasshoppers for multitude; and their camels *were* without number, as the sand by the sea side for multitude.**" God wanted it this way. God proved His power by using only three hundred men to annihilate this vastly superior multitude.

Why would God choose to achieve victory in this unlikely way? God understands the human psyche. He knew if he allowed thirty two thousand men to fight this battle and emerge victorious, some of them would be tempted to take credit for themselves. God said they might, ". . . **vaunt themselves against me (God), saying, Mine own hand hath saved me.**" (Judges 7:2).

Taking credit for our successes is the normal human tendency. Any time we experience a little success in life the temptation arises to believe our achievements are produced by our own efforts. In the case of Gideon, where only three hundred warriors are matched against one hundred fifty thousand, no one could possibly take credit. Those three hundred men knew they could never defeat a force of one hundred fifty thousand without God on their side, and so did everyone else. They were in no position to claim victory in their own strength.

35

At this point, with three hundred men huddled around Harod Spring, God's advance preparations to crush the invaders were completed; so was the transformation of Gideon into "a mighty man of valor." The idols were destroyed, and the temptation to follow the crowd was eliminated. Vigilance was the order of the day. The fourth step loomed ahead in the transformation of

Gideon from a NOBODY to a SOMEBODY. The issue
would now be obedience.

s t e p

4

Obey the Divine Directive

TO COMPLETE THIS next stage, Gideon and his reduced army must come to the REALIZATION OF THEIR FULL POTENTIALS. Gideon began this step after God spoke to him:

> ". . . Arise, get thee down unto the host; for I have delivered it into thine hand."
> (Judges 7:9)

The message was clear. The victory belonged to Gideon. God declared it, and Gideon believed it. All doubt evaporated! Since talking with the angel in the wine press, Gideon had completely changed from a

coward into a powerful man of faith. However, the Lord
suspected a trace of fear remained in Gideon's mind.
God said to him in Judges 7:10:

> **"But if thou fear to go down, go thou with
> Phurah thy servant down to the host."**

Since Gideon decided to "go down" to the Midianite
camp, some fear must have remained. God did not
condemn Gideon for being a little afraid. After all,
Gideon soon faced the greatest test of his entire life;
therefore, a twinge of fear was expected.

Even the greatest warriors experience this emotion.
For example, in 1917, Field Marshal Emile Turinne of
France stood in his tent shaving. Within moments, he
would lead the French forces into one of the most
decisive battles of World War I. Gazing at his image in
the mirror, he saw a slight tremble in his hand. He
looked down at his hand for a moment, then said: "Go
on and shake, you foul carcass. If you had any idea of
where I am about to take you, you would shake so badly
you would be unable to hold that razor at all."

The words of the Field Marshall are quite true. To
his credit, he identified the difference between his
frightened *physical nature* and his confident *spiritual
nature*. Though his physical body experienced some
degree of fear, the "real" Field Marshall Turinne (his
spirit man) experienced a surge of faith.

The <u>real</u> enemy of those standing upon God's
promises is not fear. It never has been. Fear is only a
symptom of a disease of the soul called doubt and

unbelief. Gideon experienced the former (fear), but not the latter (doubt and unbelief). Doubt is <u>always</u> unhealthy, while a little fear can sometimes be beneficial. Fear in the right doses has been known to render remarkable results.

My oldest son, Deak played football at Bishop McGuinness High School in Oklahoma City, Oklahoma. Deak was a great football player. But throughout his senior year several factors worked against him. For one thing, the McGuinness football team was young and inexperienced. There were only four starting seniors on the squad. McGuinness lost their first four games, and lost them rather badly.

Another thing working against my son was his size. Deak stood five feet seven inches tall and weighed less than 160 pounds "soaking wet." Yet he was one of the few football players in the Oklahoma City metro area playing both offense and defense. On defense he was the starting middle linebacker, and on offense he was the starting tailback. He led the entire Oklahoma City metro area in tackles and assists. That achievement was awesome in itself. In addition, he managed to become the leading offensive rusher in Oklahoma during 1985.

His most awesome accomplishment to me was the game he played against Millwood High School. It was the fifth game of the season. Millwood ranked third in the state Class 4A schools. This school produced some of Oklahoma's greatest athletes, including the great Joe Carter. Their team featured big, fast, and aggressive

athletes, and Deak knew it. In addition, he read the
Daily Oklahoman, which had established Millwood as a
seven-touchdown favorite.

On the afternoon of the game, I noticed Deak was
unusually quiet. I could see fear in his eyes. He knew
the size and toughness of the opposition. He knew they
would attempt to "shut him down." So before Deak left
for the stadium, I put my arm around his shoulder and
said: "Son, are you afraid?" He looked me right in the
eyes and said: "Just a little bit, Dad; but for some reason,
I think we're going to win this game. I can just feel it in
my bones." Yes, there was a little fear in him; but there
was no doubt.

McGuinness pulled a huge upset that night. They
played their best game of the year, winning 38 to 6.
Deak was spectacular. He rushed for 264 yards in a little
over two quarters and scored five touchdowns. He was
chosen as the "Prep Player of the Week" by the *Daily
Oklahoman.* In fact, he won several awards for his
performance against Millwood. What happened? The
shot of adrenaline produced by that touch of fear gave
him just enough of an edge to be brilliant that particular
evening.

On the other hand, if Deak had been doubtful, the
game would have been a disaster. He would have accepted the limitations of his size and the inexperience of
his team. But not Deak. He knew "CAN'T NEVER
COULD DO ANYTHING." He also knew a little fear
can be a good thing, but doubt is never good.

Gideon had a similar experience with his remaining fears, but God took these fears and used them to prop up Gideon's faith and assure his success. God said to Gideon:

> "But if thou fear to go down, go thou with Phurah thy servant . . . And thou shalt hear what they say; and afterward shall thine hands be strengthened to go down unto the host. Then went he down with Phurah his servant unto the outside of the armed men that were in the host." (Judges 7:10-11)

Notice what God did in these verses. In the first place, God did not send Gideon to the Midianite encampment alone. Certainly He could have said to Gideon: "You are a big boy now, Gideon. You need to get out there and do what I've told you to do. You've got to face it. Just suck it up and get after it. That's what a real man would do." That is never God's approach. God refused to use negative input to motivate Gideon.

Too many parents today, like my own father, choose the negative motivational approach. They say things to their children like "Can't you do anything right?" They are not being vicious toward them. They are trying to provoke their children to do things the right way, using negative motivation as the provocateur. But God motivated Gideon by using positive "can do" input. Rather than chiding Gideon for his fears, God encouraged Gideon to "take a friend" with him to the enemy encampment as a secondary means of positive reinforcement.

Gideon and his friend slipped through the darkness to the edge of the Midianite camp. There he learned another valuable lesson. To his amazement, he discovered the Midianites feared him every bit as much as he feared them. In fact, as he crawled along the perimeter of the enemy encampment, he and his friend overheard two Midianite sentries talking. One sentry shared a strange dream. In his dream, he saw a huge barley cake roll into the Midianite camp. It rolled past the campfires and into the commander's tent, overturning it. As Gideon listened, the second sentry interpreted the dream for his comrade:

> "This *is* nothing else save the sword of Gideon the son of Joash, a man of Israel: *for* into his hand hath God delivered Midian, and all the host." (Judges 7:14)

How awesome! Gideon had never been in battle. He had never led an army. Yet his enemies feared him. Overhearing this conversation must have given Gideon an enormous boost. In the best of all worlds, Gideon would not have doubted his abilities. After all, God was on his side. But Gideon was human and, like most humans who see themselves as being NOBODIES, questioned his own leadership abilities. Many negative people are assisted in overcoming their inferiority feelings by the witness of another person. In Gideon's case, the words of one of his enemies helped him recognize the SOMEBODY he was becoming. He must have been amazed his reputation had spread to the camp of his enemies.

After hearing this remarkable witness from these Midianite sentries, Gideon returned to his own encampment. He now had a plan. He knew exactly what to do to defeat his vastly superior enemy.

Gideon gathered his three hundred followers to share his battle strategy. No doubt these three hundred men anticipated some extraordinary tactics or some secret weaponry to overcome these enormous odds. When Gideon shared his plan of attack and the arms they would use, they all must have been shocked. Each man was to secure for himself a candle, an earthenware jar, and a ram's horn, or shofar.

Imagine when Gideon told them these three items would be their weapons — their only weapons. Three hundred men fighting a force of one hundred fifty thousand with nothing more than candles, jars and trumpets. No swords, no spears, no chariots — just candles, jars, and trumpets. How ridiculous! Any fool knows armed warriors cannot be defeated with trumpets, candles, and jars. After all, what kinds of weapons are these in a battle? Weapons of this type look weak and ineffective. But if the God of Israel stands behind a candle, a trumpet, and a jar, they prove to be lethal weapons, especially in the hands of righteous men.

Without question, Gideon showed enormous naivete in selecting such bizarre weaponry. The only possible explanation for his choice of weapons involved his new-found spiritual awareness. He recognized Israel's struggle was not just against Midianite invaders. The most dangerous enemies of the sons of Israel were their own negative thought lives.

At this point, Gideon learned the same truths the Apostle Paul described twelve centuries later. The great apostle wrote about warfare in his second epistle to the church in Corinth. He states:

> **"For though we walk in the flesh, we do not war after the flesh: (For the weapons of our warfare are not carnal, but mighty through God to the pulling down of strong holds;) Casting down IMAGINATIONS, and every high thing that exalteth itself against the knowledge of God, and bringing into captivity every thought to the obedience of Christ. . . ."** (II Corinthians 10:3-5) *(emphasis mine)*

As Gideon prepared to lead the attack, he was more and more certain God was fully in charge of every facet and circumstance of his life. All God required to guarantee victory for Gideon and the sons of Israel was their willingness to use these trumpets, these candles, and these jars, without regard to their natural opinion of such primitive weaponry.

Had Gideon chosen to arm his warriors with carnal weapons like swords and spears, they would have been defeated. The odds they faced were too great. So Gideon did not provide his men with carnal weapons at all. These candles, trumpets, and jars were spiritual weapons. They may have had the physical appearance of trumpets, candles, and jars, but they were more. They were weapons of faith, and they were mighty.

Without a doubt, when the followers of Gideon reassembled bearing their strange weapons, Satan whispered in their ears, "This is stupid. You are too smart to do this! What soldier would go to war holding these three 'weapons' in their hands?"

If Satan did say this, in one sense he was right. Spiritual weapons do tend to look foolish, especially to those outside the faith. For example, the Word of God tells us the act of preaching is sheer foolishness to the secular world. The very idea that the words of one solitary person about an event two thousand years ago can transform men and women seems ludicrous. Satan tries to use that idea to intimidate every preacher. He says, "Stop doing this. It is futile, useless." However, the foolishness of man proves to be the wisdom of God. Even though preaching may seem to be the most inadequate weapon imaginable in this unending struggle with Satan, a huge portion of this world has been taken from Satan by the use of the weapon of the preached Word.

In the battle Gideon's warriors faced, the key to victory was the willingness of his three hundred followers to reject conventional wisdom. They refused the temptation to focus on the inadequacy of their weapons. They willingly obeyed the instructions of their leader and divided themselves into three companies. Once they were all in the proper place, they awaited the signal to

45

attack.

When the signal came, each man did exactly as instructed. First, he sounded his trumpet. The night air filled with the eerie sounds of three hundred shofars. Once the shofars sounded, the warriors crashed their jars to the ground. Then, they picked up their burning candles, which created a eerie glow around each of them. All three hundred men yelled, "The sword of the Lord and of Gideon" (Judges 7:20).

What must not be missed is the nature of each of these "weapons" and the order in which each of these "weapons" were utilized. These three "weapons" provide a type and shadow of a New Testament reality. Also, the sequence in which they were used is revelatory. The sequence provides a vital lesson for those engaged in warfare with Satan. Warfare may involve one's own self-image or one of Satan's temptations to sin. It may involve some physical, emotional, relational, or financial dysfunction. But anyone understanding Gideon's weapons and using similar ones will experience a re-sounding victory. Here is the spiritual meaning of each of these weapons and the order in which they were used:

1) *Trumpets* — The battle commenced with the sounding of three hundred trumpets. This in itself was strange. When Gideon's warriors blew those trumpets, they took a real risk. By sounding their trumpets, they alerted their enemies. In a battle, this seems foolish. However, foolishness was of little concern to this group. After all, they were not relying on their own strength.

They stood upon God's promise of victory, so they
sounded their trumpets.

Most conservative biblical scholars recognize the
blast of a trumpet as a potent biblical symbol. A trumpet blast is often used to represent the <u>verbal</u> proclama-
tion of the Word of God. In Matthew 8, a Roman
centurion came to Jesus as He was entering the town of
Capernaum. The centurion's servant was having seizures.
The centurion asked Jesus to come help the man. Jesus
said to him, "I will come and heal him." Since Jesus of
Nazareth was God in human flesh, the promises He
uttered represent the Word of God.

The centurion must have heard some of the teach-
ings of Jesus, perhaps even a teaching similar to the one
found in Mark 11:23. There Jesus says:

> **"For verily I say unto you, That whoso-
> ever shall say unto this mountain, Be thou
> removed, and be thou cast into the sea;
> and shall not doubt in his heart, but shall
> believe that those things which he <u>saith</u>
> shall come to pass; he shall have whatso-
> ever he <u>saith</u>."** (Mark 11:23) *(emphasis
> mine)*

The centurion understood this principle because he
said to Jesus, ". . . Speak the word only and my servant
shall be healed." The centurion sounded a trumpet in a
symbolic sense. His words allowed everyone to know
exactly where he stood. This man declared for all to
hear, "I refuse to believe what my eyes see. Instead, I am
announcing to my enemies, I am declaring to the princi-

palities and powers, I believe what this man just said."

These four words, "Speak the word only," moved the heart of Jesus. He turned to the centurion and said, "Go thy way, as thou hast believed, so be it done unto thee." Matthew then reports, "And his servant was healed in the selfsame hour." A great victory came to the centurion's servant because of the words from his master's mouth.

It is not enough to pray for something. You have to speak it done as well. We must be willing to sound the trumpet if we expect any real spiritual victories in life. We must be willing to let our spiritual enemies know exactly where we stand. That is step one in achieving victory over our circumstances.

2) *Earthen Pots* — Once the trumpets sounded, Gideon's followers threw down their earthen pots with the candles inside. The followers of Gideon probably did not realize it, but the throwing down of these earthen pots provided another powerful symbol. Earthen vessels are often used in the Bible to represent human nature. Paul once spoke of a "treasure" that Christians possess in an earthen vessel. The treasure is the indwelling Christ or the person of the Holy Spirit.

In other biblical references, earthen vessels typify carnality or the fleshly nature. The fact is, before we can ever be victorious in spiritual warfare, we must crucify the human flesh by "casting it down," just as Gideon's men cast down their clay pots. Once the flesh is cast down, the spirit-man/woman is released in us and the spirit-person can go forth to do war for God effectively.

3) Candles — As the clay pots burst, Gideon's followers lifted their candles. When these candles were raised, the light shone around them. This seems strange, because this light left them fully exposed to their enemies. However, as we have seen, Gideon and his men no longer cared about being exposed. They were wholly dependent upon God for their protection, not the element of surprise. They all knew their own strength counted for nothing against the overwhelming odds, so they just allowed their lights to shine. They had become like "a city set on a hill whose light cannot be hid." Jesus later said:

> **"Let your light so shine before men, that they may see your good works, and glorify your Father which is in heaven."** (Matthew 5:16)

Gideon and all his warriors did exactly that. They allowed their light to shine and assured the victory God had promised.

This bizarre activity threw the Midianites into confusion. Gideon's battle plan succeeded. Only one other thing remained to be done before Gideon and his army could claim total victory. All he had to do was take the final step.

s t e p

5

Stand
Your
Ground

ONCE GIDEON'S FORCES sounded their trumpets, broke their jars, and took up their torches, they stood their ground. Judges 7:21 states:

> **"And they stood everyman in his place around the camp . . ."**

This final step is crucial. Many people, attempting to make the transition from feeling like a NOBODY to becoming a SOMEBODY, have victory snatched from their grasp because they fail to stand their ground. They flee in the face of victory. They flee because they are accustomed to defeat in life. They expect to lose. The idea of succeeding terrifies them. They have so few successes in life they do not recognize victory. So, rather than stepping into their victory, they retreat to the more comfortable realm of failure.

As a pastor, I have seen these useless defeats occur time and time again. I have watched as hundreds of people reach the point of overcoming their inferiority feelings, then suddenly those old fears began to rise. The process of becoming a SOMEBODY threatens them. Those old subconscious inferiority tapes play once again. With total victory in sight, they turn and run.

Several years ago, a friend campaigned for the state senate. He was an intelligent, handsome and charming person with the financial resources available to win the seat. Polls in the area indicated he would be the easy winner. As the election drew near, he experienced some familiar feelings from his past. For years he had struggled with feelings of inferiority spawned in his childhood. His fear became so strong that just before election day he withdrew his candidacy. When sure victory was in his grasp, he quit. A negative self-image stole the election from him. Standing his ground for a couple more days, he would have discovered what hundreds of other people already knew about him. He was a SOMEBODY. Everyone knew it except him.

As we have seen, overcoming negativity requires the disciplines of vigilance and determination. It demands "stickability." Those subconscious tapes will not go away. They continue to tell us we are not good enough,

52

or smart enough, or strong enough. We must reprogram our minds with SOMEBODY input, and that takes time. While the reprogramming occurs, we must stand our ground. As Paul wrote:

> **"Stand fast therefore in the liberty where-with Christ hath made us free, and be not entangled again with the yoke of bond-age."** (Galatians 5:1)

While the mind is reprogrammed, we must believe God's word and reject the faulty input of the subconscious mind. Then we will savor victory.

What if the army of Gideon had fallen back? What if they allowed the Midianites to snatch victory from the jaws of defeat? It would have been a tragedy! But many of us do just that! Christ has won complete victory over all those negative feelings residing in the subconscious mind. He gives His victory to all who believe upon Him. Therefore, we must refuse to allow those subconscious inferiority tapes to entangle us in that "yoke of bondage."

The three hundred Israelites were smart. They rejected this option. They were not about to surrender themselves to their old way of thinking. They decided to stand their ground. When they did, Judges 7:21b states:

> **"And all the host of Midian ran, and cried, and fled."**

The Midianites were now beaten. Filled with terror, they fled toward the deserts. After all, the Bible declares,

> **"Resist the devil and he will flee from**

53

you." (James 4:7)

What applies to Satan also applies to his works. When we entertain negative feelings, it is difficult to resist anything, especially temptation, because negative people always anticipate failure and inability. But when those feelings are subdued, we can begin to resist temptation. We can stand against things such as peer pressure and flawed social mores because we know the victory is ours.

Whenever the minions of Satan are resisted by warriors brandishing God's Word, these demonic foes react much like the Midianites. Judges 7:22 declares:

> " . . . and the Lord set every man's sword
> against his fellow."

In utter confusion, the Midianites turned upon one another. In their terrified state, they killed each other. Gideon's men did not have to do a thing but stand their ground. The Midianites destroyed themselves.

Whenever we resist our self-doubts and inner fears, we often find our battles take care of themselves. Many times we discover our enemies are not as awesome as we believed.

When I was a small boy, my mother required me to empty the "scraps" after supper. In the winter months, when darkness came early, I was terrified by this responsibility. As I walked to the alley where the trash cans were kept, I could see giant ogres swaying in the sky ready to pounce on me. I ran as fast as I could from the alley to my back door. The next morning the fears of the

night subsided. In the full light of day I could see the
ogres for what they really were! They were only trees and
bushes. Then, my fears would turn on themselves and
kill one another.

When a child of God stands his ground, he not only
confuses and terrifies his enemy, but OTHERS STAND
WITH HIM! Gideon witnessed this first hand when the
three hundred refused to run. They all stood their
ground. Those who had not reported for duty and the
31,700 who returned home heard of the victory, rejoined
Gideon's army "en masse," and helped them pursue
Israel's enemies. Judges 7:23 reports...

> **"And the men of Israel gathered them-
> selves together out of Naphatali, and out
> of Asher, and out of all Manasseh and
> pursued after the Midianites."**

We live in a society where people are riddled with
inferiority feelings. A vast army of people today is
awaiting the time when a righteous remnant will arise,
sound the trumpets, throw down their fleshly concerns,
and let their lights shine. They await the day the
SOMEBODIES of this world declare themselves and
march forth to subdue the enemy. People are sick of
living as NOBODIES. Two generations of Americans
have destroyed themselves by attempting to find a
chemical solution to their problems. They have destroyed their homes in their mad quest to acquire more
things. As a result, they are ruled by fear instead of
confidence. These people can become a great army if

they will throw off their chains. They might do just that if they see God's people "standing in victory."

Remember, the God of the universe witnessed to your ability to become a SOMEBODY. He did this by sending His own Son to die for you on the cross. That is how important you really are. Nothing depicts your worth more. The Son of God died for you! To understand that truth is to begin the journey to becoming a SOMEBODY.